OUTPOURINGS
OF GRACE

A selection of poems
by
Barbara Grace Skelton

Illustrations by
Anne McColl
Fraserburgh

Artwork & Graphics by
Darran Drysdale
Fraserburgh

Published by
Christian Faith Ministries
Gordon's Court
Fraserburgh
AB43 9AD
Scotland

www.cfmscotland.com

ISBN: 978-0-9561031-0-9

Barbara Skelton was born in Manchester, England and became a Christian as a child. She has been married to Keith for 42 years and they have three grown children and two grandchildren.

They have served the Lord together in pastoral and itinerant ministry all their married life.

For eight years, from 1996-2004, they served at The Open Door Church in Pennsylvania, USA where Keith was the Senior Pastor and Barbara was very active in their Ladies' Ministry.

They now enjoy a varied ministry together and count it a privilege to share God's Word both in the UK and overseas.

Dedication

This book of poems is dedicated to my beloved husband Keith, whose unfailing
love and encouragement, and many years of
Christ-centred ministry have made it possible.

It is our desire that you will catch a fresh glimpse of our
wonderful Lord Jesus and be blessed!

The poem on the following page is one I have written
as a tribute to Keith.

A JESUS FILLED LIFE

As a child he knew forgiveness from sin,
Oh what a miracle changed him within!
He heard his father the Gospel unfold,
And knew it was truth that he had been told.

All through his childhood and into his teens,
He lived for his Jesus, with all that it means.
Though tragedy touched his life whilst still young,
The song in his heart was still being sung!

Loving his family with all of his heart,
Giving his all and not just a part;
Praying and seeking the best for each one,
Doing the things that had to be done.

Called to serve Jesus, not seeking for wealth,
Blessed with a goodly measure of health;
Preaching and teaching all through the years,
Knowing peace in his sorrow and joy through his tears.

Learning to live in a world full of sin,
Showing each day that Christ was within!
Preaching Christ and His Cross, the delight of his soul,
Seeing many in Christ be changed and made whole.

A Pastor who loved the sheep in his care,
Their burdens and sorrows he gladly would share;
Desiring for Christ all the honour and glory,
A life lived for Jesus tells a wonderful story!

When sickness came to sit at his door,
Through trouble and trial, he learned to love more!
Knowing God has a purpose, he trusted the Lord,
And Jesus was still the Name he adored!

A life lived for Jesus is a bright shining light,
It glows in the darkness like a beacon at night!
It shines in this world of trouble and strife;
What value to God is a Jesus filled life!

INDEX

GRACE FOR YESTERDAY

SECTION
1

OBEDIENCE

Flesh of my flesh and bone of my bone,
Perfectly happy in Eden's new home.
Dew in the morning, stars shining at night,
Flowers and sunshine, greenery and light.
Plenty of food from Father's good hand,
Fruit on the trees and grain from the land.

How many hours was Adam away,
Naming the animals, day after day?
Elephants, tigers, pandas, giraffes,
Peacocks and pigeons, sturgeon and bass.
Not for a moment was he discontent,
Taking God with him wherever he went.

Father walked with him, they talked on the way,
Eve was fulfilled, content to obey.
Then one day when out for a stroll in the shade,
A beautiful serpent, sly overtures made.
He asked Eve the question that many repeat,
"Has God really said this?" in tones, oh, so sweet!

"If God really loved you and cared about you,
There's nothing He'd say that you couldn't do.
If God really wanted the best for your soul,
He'd give you whatever would make you feel whole.
The fruit of that tree, it looks good to eat!
Taste it and see, it looks quite a treat!"

Was Adam away or was he near home?
Wherever he was, he left Eve all alone.
Eve thought to herself, this seems to be true,
She didn't ask Adam or God what to do.
She ate some fruit from right off that tree,
And took one for Adam to have for his tea.

"Oh, Eve, my love, what's happened to you?
God's glory has gone, I see you anew.
What shall I do now, my beautiful wife?
I can't live alone for the rest of my life.
If I eat my fruit behind this big tree,
God will forgive me, He won't even see!"

Oh, Adam, your sin pays wages you know.
Your innocence, your nearness to God will go.
Yes, God really meant it when He said "don't eat,"
He asked only one thing, on that you can't cheat.
Now labour for you and pain for your Eve,
What you have done, you just can't conceive!

Oh, what will you do, friend, with my little ode?
Will you read it and think, it's too much like code?
Remember God loves you, oh, yes, this is true,
But there is one thing He wants you to do!
Obedience is key to relations with Him,
Will you open your heart and let Him come in?

Genesis 3:6
And when the woman saw that the tree was good for food, and that it was pleasant to the eyes, and a tree to be
desired to make one wise, she took of the fruit thereof, and did eat, and gave also unto her husband with her;
and he did eat.

THE SACRIFICE

Abraham and Isaac rose up early that day,
Father and son were soon on their way;
Off on their journey to worship the Lord;
Was the sacrifice more than they could afford?

Walking together, father and son,
Abraham remembered what mercy had done;
When Sarah herself failed to believe,
God intervened so that she could conceive!

Their longed-for son was there with him now,
Off to the mountain where they were to bow
To their merciful Father in Heaven above,
The One who had shown them all of His love.

Abraham believed that God's promise was true;
All God had said He surely would do!
Even from ashes on an altar of wood,
Issac would rise and go home as he should!

"Where is the lamb for the altar today?"
How would he answer, what could he say?
Two loves in his life, the Lord and his son,
Love for his God was the love that had won!

"God will provide Himself a lamb,"
Prophetic words from dear Abraham.
As Isaac was laid on an altar of love,
God had to speak from Heaven above!

"Abraham, Abraham, be sure he's not harmed,
I AM will provide, don't be alarmed!
That ram in the thicket is there just for you,
There is your sacrifice, here's what to do!

"Now I know that you love Me, my friend,
You laid down your Isaac, your love had no end!
Indeed, all the families of earth will be blessed,
You showed them the way to true holiness!"

You loved the Lord with all of your heart,
You gave Him your all, not just a part!
You trusted His promise when all appeared lost,
You worshipped the Lord, not counting the cost!

Genesis 22:2

And he said, Take now thy son, thine only son Isaac, whom thou lovest, and get thee into the land of Moriah; and offer him there for a burnt offering upon one of the mountains which I will tell thee of.

LAW AND GRACE

As Moses climbed up the mountain that day,
He had no idea how long he would stay!
He needed to worship the Lord and to pray,
For the Children of Israel were going astray!

How long it would take, he just didn't know;
What could they be doing, down there below?
He bowed in deep reverence, worship and praise,
God's glory fell down, his soul to amaze!

Day after day, night after night,
Moses was lost in that glorious sight!
God, with His finger, wrote on the stone;
The Law was given to Israel alone!

Commandments given to please God above,
To the people He chose, to kindle their love;
Laws for their lives that must be obeyed,
Laws of His righteousness here were displayed!

Carefully descending, stones in his hands,
Moses went back to Aaron as planned!
Aaron had betrayed his heart and his soul,
Listening to complaints, he put their god on a pole!

How could he do this terrible thing?
An image of gold made from all their earrings;
"This is your god who delivered you here,
This is the god whom you must fear!"

For their sinful behaviour and idolatrous ways,
God's anger was kindled against them for days!
Moses pleaded with God that his friends would be saved;
His anger abated, though they were depraved!

When Moses saw the depth of their sin,
He threw down the stones, anger burning within!
"Nehushtan" piece of brass, he exclaimed loud and clear,
Then he ground it to powder, made them tremble with fear!

They paid the price of disobedience that day;
Many were killed, lost their lives in the fray!
Moses went into God's house for to hear,
The Lord speak to him as a friend drawing near!

"Show me Your glory, show me Your way,
Have mercy upon me, Lord, hear what I say!
I cannot go on without You, dear Lord;
These people I lead are not in accord!"

"I cannot do this, Moses, my friend,
You would not live, your life would just end!
If you hide in the rock, My face I will veil,
You can trust Me, my friend, I AM will not fail!"

"Back up the mountain, alone you must go,
There I will meet you, My glory I'll show!"
God wrote His commandments again with His hand;
Obedience was God the Father's demand.

The tablets of stone were put in their place,
Laid in the Mercy Seat, covered by grace!
God's justice and mercy for ever enshrined,
Jehovah and Israel for ever entwined!

Deuteronomy 10:5
And I turned myself and came down from the mount, and put the tablets in the ark which I had made; and there
they be, as the Lord commanded me.

BEFORE THE ALTAR

Zacharias come quickly, it's time to go,
You cannot be late; don't be so slow!
It's the moment you've waited for all of these years,
Now isn't the time to have any fears!
Once in a lifetime, what an honour for you,
Remember, Zacharias, your vows to renew!

All this time you have served the Lord,
He's the One you have loved, the One you've adored!
Do your duty today, as you always must do,
Then tell Him you love Him and worship Him too!
Be cleansed and sanctified to the Lord today,
And tell Him your sadness, Zacharias, I pray!

Before the altar Zacharias soon stood,
Offering incense as the Law said he should!
Then, there in the Temple, an angel appeared,
The old man was startled and shook, for he feared!
"Don't be afraid," God has heard your prayer,
The son that you've longed for, Elizabeth will bear!

He will be great and will bring you great joy,
He'll be separate and special, God's little boy!
Chosen to prepare the way for the Lord,
Filled with the Spirit, powerful, assured!
Just like Elijah, he'll turn hearts right around,
Just like Elijah, God's message he'll sound!

How old am I? How can this be?
Elizabeth's too old to have a child with me!
We've waited so long, prayed and prayed for a son,
It's hard to believe that this thing can be done!
The time has passed by; how all those years flew!
Why wait until now for our dreams to come true?

"Zacharias, why don't you believe in my word?
Why can't you accept all the things you have heard?
I would not lie before the altar today;
You will not speak until I have my way!
Finish your service, go home to your wife,
Wait for a miracle of love in your life!"

He returned to Elizabeth, unable to speak,
No longer doubting, but humble and meek!
Elizabeth conceived and bare him a son,
No more reproach, but respect could be won!
"His name will be John" as the angel had shared!
Zacharias spoke, as God's Word he declared!

My wonderful Jesus lives in Heaven for me,
Before His high throne of great majesty!
I have one defence: I have only one plea,
My Saviour's shed blood on Calvary's Tree!
Praise God, He is living to set me free!
My faithful, merciful High Priest is He.

Luke 1:13
But the angel said unto him, Fear not Zacharias: for thy prayer is heard; and thy wife Elizabeth shall bear thee a son, and thou shalt call his name John.

CHOSEN

Now the birth of Christ was on this wise,
Godlessness was on the rise,
The prophets were no longer heard,
When God gave us the Living Word!

Laws and Feasts were still observed,
Past traditions were preserved.
Messiah would come to be their King,
His coming would change everything!

The Romans had occupied their land,
The Jews had suffered at their hand!
In this their time of deep distress,
God revealed His holiness!

A maiden, starting out in life,
Betrothed to be dear Joseph's wife,
One day a heavenly angel heard,
Bringing her a prophetic word!

A chosen vessel in God's plan,
To bring God's mercy down to man!
This highly favoured child of thine,
Would bear the Holy Seed Divine!

Mary surrendered herself to God's will,
Father had promised her being to fill!
What would dear Joseph think of her now?
He'd surely believe she'd broken her vow!

She went to her cousin up in the hills,
Maybe she'd share with her all that God wills.
As soon as they met and shared an embrace,
Elizabeth greeted her, looked in her face.

Sharing with joy all that Mary had heard,
Mary rejoiced in the honour conferred.
Shame and disgrace, she surely would share,
Counting it loss, Messiah to bear!

God sent an angel to Joseph and said,
"Fear not, dear Joseph, your Mary to wed!
She's not been unfaithful, this babe is from Me!
Mary is chosen salvation to see!"

Caesar Augustus sent out a decree,
The world would be taxed by each family.
Joseph and Mary to Bethlehem went,
To register in David's line of descent.

It was time for Mary to deliver her child,
No room could be found for this babe meek and mild!
A stable was offered and manger so lowly,
How could it hold an infant so holy?

As Mary looked into the eyes of her son,
How could she know all that God had begun?
That baby so helpless, fragile and small,
Would grow to become the Saviour of all!

Much joy He would bring her, this little life.
Such sorrow and anguish, such pain and such strife!
There never had been a baby like this,
How could she know as she gave Him a kiss?

Shepherds, then wise men, in worship bowed down,
God's glory was born, right there in that town!
Mary kept all of this deep in her heart,
What of His future, would she have a part?

As Simeon, the prophet of God, now declared,
This was the baby that God had prepared.
Mary a chosen vessel so fair,
Christ was chosen our sins for to bear!

Luke 1:30-31
And the angel said unto her, Fear not, Mary: for thou hast found favour with God. And, behold, thou shalt
conceive in thy womb, and bring forth a son, and shalt call his name JESUS.

MARY'S CHILD

As Mary looked on her son that day,
Sleeping there on a new bed of hay,
Her fingers gently stroked His sweet brow,
As she wondered what would become of Him now.

Those swaddling bands wound around Him so tight;
What was He dreaming of all through the night?
She was so young and He was so small,
Messiah laid there in an animal's stall!

What if she dropped Him? What if He should fall?
Would she be faithful? Would He grow to be tall?
Would she be able to care for this Child?
This innocent baby, so meek and so mild!

The Word born as flesh, right here and right now!
Born to be King with a crown on His brow!
What kind of king is this baby of mine?
King of the Jews who is also divine!

This baby born to be Saviour of all,
Would know adoration before He could crawl.
The Shepherds were first to bring Him their love,
Bowing their knees to the Lamb from above!

Wise men from the East brought gifts to His feet,
Gold, Frankincense, Myrrh, their Saviour to greet;
A sweet smelling savour to Father above,
For the wonderful, glorious gift of His love!

Angels were amazed to see Him lie there,
They hovered around and lingered to stare.
"Worship Him now" was the Father's command,
They'd never seen God wrapped in tight swaddling bands.

Mary pondered these things deep down in her heart,
She knew He was special, right from the start.
Words of the prophets fulfilled there that night,
Soon she and Joseph would have to take flight!

All through His childhood her baby grew well,
As for His future, she just couldn't tell.
Mary and Joseph were never alone,
For God lived with them, right there in their home!

Her son grew so strong, went to die on a tree,
For Joseph and Mary and sinners like me!
Will you give Him your worship and love, oh, my friend?
From the crib to the Cross, His love has no end!

Luke 2:7
And she brought forth her firstborn son, and wrapped him in swaddling clothes, and laid him in a manger;
because there was no room for them in the inn.

WHY

Enthroned in glorious majesty,
In light no mortal eye could see!
Creator of the world and sky,
What made You come to earth to die?

You spoke the word, the earth was formed,
At Your command, the first day dawned!
You separated land and sea,
What made You come to die for me?

From dust You formed the earth's first man,
Male and female, in His plan;
They ate from the forbidden tree;
What made You come to set us free?

They sinned and sinned, and sinned again!
You sent the flood to ease Your pain!
A rainbow showed Your grace prevailed!
Why did You save us when we failed?

The patriarchs and prophets came,
Preaching Your Word, proclaiming Your Name!
Men would not hear; preferred a lie!
Why did You leave Your home on high?

No Word of God for many years,
The angel Gabriel then appears,
A Jewish maid You chose to bless!
Why did You come with tenderness?

God's Son, who was given "a wonderful name!"
Made lower than angels, to a virgin You came,
To a manger in Bethlehem's poverty!
Why did You come with humility?

You lived on earth, died on a tree,
Upon the cruel Cross of Calvary!
God's love displayed for all to see:
Why did You give Yourself for me?

Love made You come from Heaven's glory!
Love made You write redemption's sweet story;
Love made You die on a cruel wooden tree!
Love paid the ransom for sinners like me!

John 1:3
All things were made by him; and without him was not any thing made that was made.

DAY OF MIRACLES

Why did they follow Him over the sea?
Why did they go there without any tea?
What had they seen to urge them along?
What was their reason for joining the throng?
For thirty-eight years the man had lain there,
By the pool of Bethesda, deep in despair!

What wonderful words he heard there that day.
"Rise, take up your bed, and walk on your way!"
Though many disputed his right to arise,
He picked up his bed in front of their eyes!
He told all around what Jesus had done;
The multitude listened and followed God's Son!

Passover time was now drawing near,
No food could be bought, that was now clear.
All of these people, where could they find bread?
The Lord had the answer, He knew they'd be fed.
Then out of the crowd came one little lad,
Five loaves and two fishes was all that he had!

All he had to give was the bread of the poor,
He gave what he had and couldn't give more!
They were asked to sit down, line upon line,
The people were fed time after time!
As much as you want, eat what you will,
Jesus has plenty of bread for you still!

The leftover food, it must not be waste,
Don't leave it behind in all of your haste!
Put it in baskets, you'll see what is there,
Be careful they're not too heavy to bear.
Twelve baskets were left and everyone fed!
How could this be, from those fish and that bread?

Oh, wonder of wonders, what Jesus can do!
Could all of these miracles really be true?
Could a lame man walk and five thousand be fed?
All with a little boy's fishes and bread?
What more can He do, this Jesus we love?
He's really God's Son, come down from above!

The Lord went up into the mountain to pray,
They went out to sea at the end of the day.
The storm rocked their boat, the Lord saw their plight,
He walked on the water and gave them a fright!
"Lord is it you?" brave Peter called out,
"Yes, it is I," there's no need to doubt!

"Walk on the water and come to Me here,
Get out of the boat, don't have any fear!"
In faith, Peter stepped right into those waves,
He found that his Jesus was the Jesus who saves!
When he reached out to Jesus and took hold of His hand,
He was back in the boat and soon on dry land.

The people were amazed, where could he be?
How did he get there across that rough sea?
What can we do, Lord, to work out God's will?
What can we do God's law to fulfil?
Believe on me, the Bread from above,
I Am has come down to bring you God's love!

John 6:9
There is a lad here, which hath five barley loaves, and two small fishes: but what are they among so many?

17

WHEN GOD RAN

My father's house was rich indeed,
All I could want or ever need.
His love had overflowed to me,
I was his beloved son, you see!

Though all my future seemed secure,
I could not keep from wanting more.
In my heart I made this vow,
I would ask for all my money now!

Father wept when he heard me say,
I want my inheritance today!
I'll have my share so that I can go;
I want to see the world, you know!

I heeded not his pain or tears,
Did not care about his fears!
I took from him all I was due,
And disappeared right out of view!

Off to enjoy my father's wealth,
Didn't care about my health!
Didn't even turn to see,
My father weeping over me!

Enjoy myself? Oh, yes, I did,
It wasn't that I went and hid.
I had the life folks dream about,
But somehow things did not work out!

It wasn't very long before,
I spent it all, I had no more!
My friends all left me on my own,
No one around to hear my moan!

I had to find some way to eat,
Some way to keep me on my feet.
A farmer said, "Go feed the swine."
A Jewish boy, what shame was mine!

Almost too late, it dawned on me,
The thing that I could never see.
My father's heart was kind and true,
I knew right then what I must do.

I must go back to my father's home,
Why, oh why, did I ever roam?
His servants never want for bread,
How long is it since I was fed?

I trudged back on my weary way,
It seemed forever and a day.
Then in the distance there I saw,
The place that I'd been longing for!

I'm so tired I can hardly see,
But who's that running down to me?
After all the things I've done,
Why would anybody run?

Now I see. Could this be right?
Oh, what a joy; oh, what delight!
Instead of leaving me to roam,
My father's come to take me home!

I'm so ashamed of what I've done,
But father treats me like a son!
He puts his arms around me tight,
Weeps tears of joy, keeps me in sight!

A robe, a ring and shoes for me,
All his treasures full and free!
I don't deserve his tender care,
He showed to me a love most rare!

A feast is spread to celebrate,
But who's that frowning by the gate?
My older brother isn't pleased,
I do not think he'll be appeased!

After all, my sin was great,
I couldn't blame him for his hate!
My father saw him in distress,
And spoke to him with tenderness!

"My son, all that I have is thine,
Yours is the right to come and dine!
When all of this is said and done,
There's plenty left for you, my son!"

In my Father's bounteous love,
He's prepared my home above
The day my journey home began,
My Father looked on me, AND RAN!

Luke 15:18-19
I will arise and go to my father, and will say unto him, Father, I have sinned against heaven, and before thee, And am no more worthy to be called thy son…

THE HUSBANDMAN

As the husbandman walked through the vines on the hill,
The sight of them there gave his heart such a thrill;
As he looked on their glory by morning light,
He could not conceal his joy and delight!

He'd planted them there when they were so small,
Now they'd grown quite strong and they were so tall!
Row after row up the hill they were lined,
He'd tended them all with fruit on his mind!

The soil was so special, just right for his trees,
It had taken so long for the compound to please!
His vines needed nourishment right from the ground,
He had to be sure the best soil was found!

Sometimes too wet, and sometimes too dry.
Over and over he'd just had to try.
Weeds would spring up each time he turned round,
He'd certainly laboured to till all that ground!

The roots he had planted took well on the land,
Though tangled and twisted and wound all around,
They were healthy and able to draw from the soil,
A tribute indeed to the husbandman's toil!

When foxes had tried their roots to devour,
He'd watched for his vines, stayed hour after hour!
Protecting them from all evil intent,
Hour after hour round his vineyard he went!

Day after day he'd looked after his vines,
Searching to detect the smallest of signs.
Is this branch diseased? Could this one be bruised?
Over and over on each one he mused!

When one branch had broken and needed some care,
He'd bound it and propped it, the burden to bear!
Some branches he'd pruned, some more he had spliced,
But only the sap from the vine had sufficed!

The leaves were so green now, the blossoms so bright.
They danced in the breeze and shone in the light!
The sight of his vineyard rewarded his toil,
Nothing and no one this moment could spoil!

Now was the season for fruit to appear,
The time for harvest soon would draw near:
Succulent fruit would hang from each bough,
Soon he would savour the work of his brow!

My Heavenly Father has planted a vine;
His Son is the stem and the root so divine!
We are the branches, partakers of love,
Sustained and revived by His life from above.

He's planted each one where He wants us to grow,
He tends us and prunes us and wants us to know,
When we are obedient and honour His Word,
Our fruit will abound and bring praise to our Lord!

John 15:1
I am the true vine, and my Father is the husbandman.

GOD WHO KNEW

God, who did not spare His Son,
But gave to us the Holy One;
Gave Him with a heart of love,
Sent Him from His home above,
Down to this old sinful earth,
Because He knew your soul's true worth.

God, who could not bear to see,
The sin laid on His Son for me;
Turned away His face from Him,
Wrapped darkness round that place for Him;
Heard Him cry, "Oh, Father, why
Can I not see You as I die?"

God, who watched as Mary cried,
Watched as John went to her side;
Saw the soldiers stand and jeer,
Saw His friends all flee in fear;
Saw the grave, the stone, the seal,
Knew that Satan's power was real!

God, who knew His Son would win,
That final battle over sin;
Knew the keys of death would be,
Taken there for all to see!
Raised His Son up from the grave,
Showed the world His power to save!

God, who planned this with His Son,
Rejoiced with Him when it was done;
Crowned Him with the victor's crown,
Sent the Holy Spirit down,
To be our Comforter and Friend,
Our broken hearts and minds to mend.

THE PASSOVER LAMB

Passover time had come at last,
The meal was ready, the die was cast.
They came to remember mercy that night,
Here was the Lamb before them, in sight!

Down through the ages remembrance was made,
The blood on the doorposts, the price that was paid.
They drank of four cups and ate of the bread,
The lamb on the plate showed the blood to be shed!

There was one at the table who knew naught of the Lamb,
He ate and he drank, but he had his own plan.
Treated as honoured! what must he have thought?
He must have considered he'd never be caught!

Time in the feast to drink the third cup,
The cup of Redemption, would He drink it all up?
"This is My blood," He said to each friend,
They never envisaged this might mean the end!

The end of His life on the earth He created,
The end of the Lamb, whom the people had feted.
He spoke about love and the kingdom to come,
They sang the Hallel, the meal almost done.

At the end of the meal, the Lamb took a bowl,
And washing their feet, took a Servant's role:
Stooping, the Lamb could not bend any lower,
He did it to show humility's power.

Walking through streets where the vines were in bloom,
Straight to the Garden, His agony soon!
Here was the Lamb, perfect sacrifice come,
To give of His all, Oh! worship the Lamb!

Soon in the Glory the feast will be spread,
The Bride at the table, the Lamb at the head;
The cup of Redemption we'll drink there anew,
Remember the Lamb, He suffered for you!

Luke 22:19-20
And he took bread, and gave thanks, and brake it, and gave unto them, saying, This is my body which is given for you: this do in remembrance of me. Likewise also the cup after supper, saying, This cup is the new testament in my blood, which is shed for you.

WITNESSES

The Lord said, "Come up the mountain to pray;"
That was the Lord's invitation that day:
We climbed up together following our Jesus,
Then Moses and Elijah came right there to meet us!

They'd been gone for years, so how could this be?
But there they were for us, plainly to see!
Shocked and amazed, knowing not what to say,
We thought we would talk to the Lord anyway!

"Let's build a memorial for each of you here,"
Elijah and Moses might soon disappear!
One for you too, Lord, we can't forget you,
We really don't know just what we should do!

The Law and the Prophets, that was God's way,
The Children of Israel had been led till that day.
We wanted to keep them right there in that place,
We needed to remember all of God's grace!

Father could keep His silence no more,
He spoke from the Glory with voice strong and sure.
"This is My Son" right there with you now,
HE is the One to whom you must bow!

Humanities chrysalis broken in two,
His heavenly glory came into our view!
Transfigured before us in glory so bright,
The essence of Jesus shone forth in great light!

Falling before Him, dumbfounded, as dead,
Jesus came to us, knowing our dread.
Our wonderful Lord, so tender and wise,
Took pity upon us and said, "Friends, arise!"

As we rose to our feet, still trembling with fear,
Only our Jesus was still standing near.
Elijah and Moses had gone from our sight;
Leaving Jesus to make everything right.

He told us quite plainly, "I will arise,
Go back to My Father, My home in the skies.
Do not speak of what happened here today,
I'll go back to My Father, just as I say."

Our minds were darkened and we could not see,
We had no idea what the future would be.
We certainly never considered a cross,
Or know that soon we would suffer such loss!

But we were Your witnesses, Lord, in this place;
We saw Your glory, Your beauty and grace!
Your majesty left us in no doubt at all,
That You were our Lord and the Saviour of all!

2 Peter 1:16
…but (we) were eyewitnesses of his majesty.

27

MARY'S CROSS

With trembling hands she wiped her eyes,
And looking upward to the skies,
She prayed with heartfelt grief and pain,
"Oh, Father, glorify Your Name,
But that's my son hanging from that tree,
Please, Father, take him down for me?

"I just can't stand to see him there,
This awful sight is too hard to bear!"
"Oh, Father, I loved him right from the start!
Before he was born he captured my heart.
Hanging there in such grief and shame,
How can a cross glorify Your Name?

"Father, why does he have to suffer so much,
He needs Your help and Your tender touch!"
His hands healed the sick, made blind eyes to see,
Made lame men to walk and comforted me!
He only gave hope and healing and joy,
He was such a delight, he was my little boy!

"My firstborn son hanging there in such shame!
The One who was given a Wonderful Name!
The promised Messiah, The Prince of Peace!
The One to bring captives such sweet release!
Born to be King and reign over the Jews,
For His chosen people, what glorious news!

"What grief is mine on this terrible day!"
What an awful price my son has to pay!
A lamb to the slaughter, He did not protest,
An innocent dying for the sin of the rest!
The Passover lamb makes atonement for me,
Buying redemption on Calvary's tree!

"Oh, Father, this must be what You had planned,
Though I must confess, I don't understand!"
His friends and disciples are all gone away,
They fear for their lives on this heartrending day!
Those who love most could not leave Him alone,
He is flesh of my flesh and bone of my bone!

"A mother's hopes and dreams are crushed,
My heart lies broken in the dust,
Messiah hangs for all to see,
Love's sacrifice on Calvary!
And yet I know that it is true,
He made this sacrifice for you!"

John 19:25
Now there stood by the cross of Jesus his mother…

AN EMPTY TOMB

We sat and watched as they laid Him there,
Our hearts were so heavy it was too much to bear!
Joseph wrapped Him and laid Him there in his tomb,
That evening was filled with darkness and gloom!
No time to anoint Him for Sabbath was nigh,
What a terrible way for my Jesus to die!

We returned to the garden when Sabbath was o'er,
But how will we roll the stone from the door?
The earth shook so much, we trembled with fright,
And an angel appeared in glorious light!
"Why look for the living among the dead,
He's not here, He is risen," the angel said!

We ran to our friends to tell them the news;
They didn't believe us, they had their own views!
So Peter ran quickly to the grave just to see,
If the things we had told him could possibly be!
The grave clothes lay there, all folded and neat,
And I saw two angels at the head and the feet!

With tears in my eyes, I saw Him stand there,
I did not know Him, the sight was so rare:
"They've taken the body of my Lord away,
Oh, tell me where you have laid Him I pray!"
I'm just overwhelmed with grief and pain,
For I watched as my wonderful Jesus was slain!

I knew it was Him when He spoke out my name;
From the first time I met Him, I'd not been the same!
He'd changed my life, made me whole, set me free;
Could this be the One who was speaking to me?
"Rabboni" I cried in worship and praise,
My Lord you're alive! Stay here whilst I gaze!

"Mary, don't be afraid, go tell all My friends,
Come and meet me in Galilee: This isn't the end!
Tell Peter to come for I want him to know,
I'm going to My Father and I still love him so!
I have told you these things, My Word is still true;
All I have promised I surely will do!"

All the disciples gathered together that day,
They met in secret to talk and to pray!
Afraid of the Jews, they locked all the doors,
This was no problem to Christ, that's for sure!
He spoke words of peace, showed His hands and His feet,
Convincing them all, their Saviour to greet!

Thomas was absent and could not believe,
"I must see for myself, I just can't conceive!"
So wonderful Jesus appeared once again,
For Thomas to see the marks of His pain;
"Thomas, you have seen Me, so now you believe,
Blessed are those who My Spirit receive!"

The disciples went fishing, toiled all through the night,
Catching nothing, they came to the shore at first light:
The risen Christ met them, "Drop your nets on that side,"
The nets were soon filled with Christ as their guide!
He proved beyond doubt, He is risen from the tomb!
Our living Lord Jesus will return for us soon!

Matthew 28:6

He is not here: for he is risen, as he said…

WE'VE JUST SEEN JESUS!

Our feet were heavy as we walked on our way:
The awful events of the previous days,
Were seared on our minds, we would never forget,
His anguish and pain, the blood and the sweat!
Beaten and scourged, then hung on a tree,
Dying in shame for all men to see:
Our wonderful Jesus, who made our hearts sing!
Bethlehem's Babe who was born to be King.

What cowards we were, now ashamed and cast down,
We just couldn't stop them, they gave Jesus that crown.
A crown of thorns that pierced His sweet brow:
Oh! what would our Jesus think of us now?
We were all afraid; thinking "this could be me"
The fear gripped our hearts; it was all we could see.
We cowered in corners, fled out of the way:
It was too much to bear, we just couldn't stay!

He was God's Prophet, so certain were we,
The Promised Redeemer come to set us all free:
Now, even His body has gone from the tomb,
And all of our joy has turned to dark gloom.
A stranger joined us as we walked on our way,
He asked us about the news of that day:
We could not believe that he did not know,
The tragic events that had brought our hearts low!

When we had finished our story of woe,
The stranger spoke up and admonished us so;
Surely you know what the Prophets have said?
Surely you've heard, have you not read?
He expounded to us the truth of God's Word,
Concerning Messiah, the true Son of God:
His suffering and pain, the infinite cost,
Our Redeemer would pay to buy back the lost!

Then at last we had reached our journey's end,
We were sorry to leave our kind gentle friend;
So we asked him if he would abide in our home,
For nightfall had come, it was not safe to roam.
There was something about the way that he prayed,
We took notice of him when his hands were displayed;
There was something about the way he broke bread,
We suddenly knew, Christ was risen from the dead!

Just as we pondered what we should do,
He vanished completely, right out of our view;
In joyous amazement we cried and we talked,
Turning back down the road that we had just walked,
How could we know what all this might mean?
Was this really our Jesus alive from the dead?
We tried to remember all the things he had said.

When we got back to tell all of our friends,
It seemed that the news of that day had no end!
Peter had seen the Lord whom he loved;
They did not believe it, "How could it be proved?"
Then Jesus Himself appeared to us there,
They were words of peace that He had to share.
See My hands, see My feet, touch My body to see,
A spirit does not have flesh and bones like Me!

He proved beyond doubt He was raised from the dead,
Our wonderful Jesus came back as He said.
Our heavy hearts were thrilled with great joy,
Nothing in this world our faith could destroy!
What things lay ahead, no one could tell,
But we had seen Jesus, we knew very well;
Messiah had come, His Word came to pass,
The Law was fulfilled in our Jesus at last!

Luke 24:31
And their eyes were opened, and they knew him; and he vanished out of their sight.

FAITHFUL

Since God created time and space,
Since He first hung the stars in place,
His love and faithfulness to man,
Has been a part of His great plan.

To men and women through the years,
Who've trusted God despite their fears,
He's given the joy and peace of mind,
That He would give to all mankind!

When Abel offered up his lamb
To God, who is the great "I AM",
His faithful sacrifice that day,
Showed Cain had turned his heart away!

Old Enoch chose to walk with God,
With prayer and faith, his feet were shod:
One day, God said to him, "Come home,
There's no more need for you to roam."

When Noah's Ark appeared insane,
"A boat to save us from the rain!"
He warned them all that they would drown,
Though not a drop of rain came down!

Abraham left his home and land,
To go to a place that God had planned:
Receiving God's promise, he believed it was true,
Whatever God wanted, Abraham would do!

When he was tested to give up his son,
He surrendered his Isaac, the deed almost done;
Refusing to doubt, he chose to believe,
Knowing his Father would never deceive!

Joseph made certain the future was planned,
His bones must go up to the Promised Land:
Moses refused all the pleasures of sin,
Preferring affliction, God's favour to win!

By faith, Moses sprinkled the Passover blood,
By faith, he stood where no man had stood!
He crossed the Red Sea walking over dry land,
God parted the waters by His powerful hand.

Day after day as they marched around each wall,
Joshua believed that soon they would fall:
Rahab believed when she hung out that cord,
That Jehovah God was a God of His Word!

Many ordinary people with faith in their God,
Willingly suffered on the path that they trod:
In weakness they were strong; in trials brave,
Refusing deliverance their witness to save!

They were mocked and beaten and ridiculed too,
Stoned and killed, yet they believed God was true!
Destitute, tormented, without homes, without land,
How could this be what their Father had planned?

Yet, they kept the faith, never knowing "the why"
They may never have known why they had to die!
Given no reasons for their suffering and pain,
Believing that Heaven was the "glory" to gain!

These wonderful witnesses, gone on ahead,
Watch now as we walk down the road that we tread,
They inspire our hearts to trust You today,
And encourage us all to be faithful and pray.

Hebrews 12:1
Wherefore seeing we also are compassed about with so great a cloud of witnesses, let us lay aside every weight,
and the sin which doth so easily beset us, and let us run with patience the race that is set before us.

... AND FOR TODAY

SECTION

2

BEHOLD HIM

Before time was or the earth was formed,
Before light or space or the first day had dawned;
Before the first man was clothed or shod,
The Word was in Heaven, the Word was God!

Disentangling Himself from His Father above,
He descended through angels to bring us God's love!
He planted Himself in Mary's young womb,
Knowing His love would end in a tomb!

Born as a baby in Bethlehem's stall,
The Creator of Nature became Saviour of all!
Behold this babe, and looking please see,
That Christ put Himself there, for you and for me!

Submitting Himself to parental control,
Growing to love them with all of His soul;
Behold this Child, and looking please see,
He learned the obedience to die on a Tree!

Behold the Man, raise Lazarus from the dead,
Behold the Man, as five thousand are fed!
Behold the Man, and looking please see,
He died on the Cross so that you could go free!

Behold the Conqueror arise the third day!
Behold your Saviour in glorious array!
Behold your King, and looking please see,
He's the King of all Glory by Royal decree!

Lord, what kind of love is this,
That gave a guilty world a kiss?
Love made a plan to rescue me,
Before I was or ere could be.
What kind of love left Heaven's glory
Stooping to write Redemption's story?

What kind of love became a man?
Creator God, You made a plan!
The One who set the stars in place,
And made the world and time and space,
Became the seed in Mary's womb;
Was born to die, rise from a tomb!

What kind of love would give me breath,
But for Himself choose cruel death?
What kind of love brings hope and peace,
But for Himself plans no release?
What kind of love brought liberty,
But He, Himself, would not go free?

What kind of love would share with me,
The treasure of divinity?
The apple of Your Father's eye,
What kind of love would make You die,
That awful death on Calvary,
And die to save someone like me?

What kind of love do I give to You?
Can You be seen in all I do?
When I look inside my heart,
And search to see if You've a part,
With all my heart and mind and soul,
I pray that You will have the whole!

1 John 3:1
Behold, what manner of love the Father hath bestowed upon us, that we should be called the sons of God…

I'm covered by mercy and saved by your grace,
I'm always enfolded within your embrace;
Your eyes, full of love, look down upon me,
The loved one you died for on Calvary's Tree!

My name is engraved on Your heart and Your hands,
I dress in your righteousness, God's just demands!
You hold forth Your sceptre and bid me to come
Into Your presence, oh, Most Holy One!

Your hands and Your feet bear the marks of the nails,
Bearing witness to all that Your blood still avails!
Those hands healed the sick and raised up the dead,
Made blind eyes to see and multiplied bread!

Your feet brought good news, the Gospel of peace;
From sin's cruel bondage, You brought sweet release!
You walked on this earth and walked on the sea,
Then Your feet walked the road to Calvary for me!

Psalm 23:6
Surely goodness and mercy shall follow me all the days of my life...

The morning sun broke through each cloud,
My heart and soul and thoughts were bowed;
I'd come into the Secret Place,
Where I found love and peace and grace:
All that I had I came to bring,
Into the presence of the King!

No royal robe had I to wear,
No crown to grace my head and hair,
No costly ring, no jewels fine;
No gifts of gold or food or wine:
When I looked in My Saviour's face,
All I possessed was Sovereign Grace!

What could I bring my Royal Host,
I had no wealth of which to boast!
Oh, what delight to hear Him say,
"My child, I want to hear you pray!"
Obedience, love and praise please bring,
Into the presence of Your King!

Sit at My table, come and dine!
All the wealth I have is thine!
Though you are poor and weak and lame,
I will receive you just the same!
I'll clothe you with My righteousness,
More glorious than a royal dress!

Sitting there with faults and fears,
All my lameness disappears!
My poverty, You do not see,
Your eyes are moved with love for me;
A heart of praise I gladly bring,
Into the presence of My King.

SORROW'S DOOR

When sorrow comes to sit at my door,
The sun and the moon don't shine any more,
When day seems like night and night seems like day,
My heart wants to run and just hide away.
Where can I go to find rest for my soul?
Where can I go to make me feel whole?

Should I go to the world with its sham and its shame?
Should I look to great writers or poets of fame?
Should I look to my family, they are so dear?
Should I look to my friends who are always near?
Should I look to great riches or stock market gain?
Should I look to myself with all of my pain?

Is there peace to be found in this old world of ours?
When troubles come down and fall just like showers?
Is there hope in psychology, science or art?
Is there joy that is lasting for my aching heart?
Is there peace in a world torn by trouble and strife?
Is there yet any hope for those seeking life?

I will look in the face of my Saviour above,
As He binds up my wounds with a bandage of love.
I will look to the Cross where my Saviour divine
Took all of my sorrow and the sin that was mine.
Where should I look to mend my poor heart?
I will look to the Lamb, Lord, how precious Thou art!

My Father graciously stoops to feed me,
When I am lost, He gently leads me!
When I fall down, He raises me up;
When I am thirsty, I drink from His cup!

His cords of love and kindness hold me,
Near to His heart, where He gently enfolds me!
He bears my burden and lets me know,
That His grace and mercy to me overflow!

I am His child, His joy, His delight,
Pleased when I praise Him, He keeps me in sight!
When worship flows from deep in my heart,
Nothing on earth can keep us apart.

When I fail and cause His heart to ache,
He forgives my sin for Jesus' sake;
He tenderly helps me to see when I'm wrong,
And I fly to His presence, where I belong!

He bids me dwell in the shadow of His wings,
Safely protected by the King of all kings!
No arrows of day, no perils of night,
No malice or fear can put me to flight!

When I spend myself and I am spent,
He gathers a harvest and makes me content.
His goodness and kindness to me are made plain,
When I seek to bless others in His precious Name!

Psalm 23:1
The LORD is my shepherd; I shall not want.

Being in the attitude to glorify God's Son,
Hearts are filled with joy and peace, not in the things we've done!
But in our heart's devotion and obedience to God's Word
Christ is always lifted up, He's worshipped and adored!

Being poor in spirit and saying no to I,
Makes us more like Jesus, stops us asking why!
Hungering and thirsting for this paucity of pride,
Leaves no room for selfishness or make-believe inside!

Being in the attitude of those whom You call meek,
Makes us Your inheritors and we Your glory seek!
Your Spirit works within us, showing us each flaw,
We become Your peacemakers, preferring peace to war!

Being in the attitude of those whose hearts are pure,
We see You just a little, and always long for more!
We know that we must seek You, with heart and mind and soul,
Then, and only then we find, You satisfy the whole!

Being always merciful, we glorify Your Name,
We obtain Your mercy, You set our hearts aflame!
Hearts beat with Your tenderness, eyes are moist with tears,
We see our own unworthiness, our failings and our fears!

Being sometimes persecuted, showing Christ this way,
We know that He bends down His ear to listen as we pray.
The servant cannot be above the master, whom he serves,
We know His love, His peace and grace, much more than we deserve!

The way we live our lives each day, the way that we behave,
The things we give our lives to, the things that our hearts crave;
The place we store our treasure, on earth or heaven above,
Demonstrates to everyone, the person that we love!

Matthew 5:3
Blessed are the poor in spirit: for theirs is the kingdom of heaven.

Having been into Your presence,
Having worshipped at Your throne,
Having seen Your grace and mercy,
Having claimed You for my own,
How could I exist without You?
How could I exist alone?

Having set my face to serve You,
Having followed in Your plan,
Having fallen and been lifted,
Having seen Your guiding hand,
How could I seek other, Master?
How could I be proud or grand?

Having tasted of Your goodness,
Having wondered at Your love,
Having gloried in forgiveness,
Having felt Your Spirit move,
How could I not seek Your glory?
How could I offend Your dove?

Alabaster jar of worship,
Alabaster jar of prayer,
Alabaster jar of service,
Alabaster jar, so rare.
May it smell to You, Lord, sweet,
As I bathe Your glorious feet.

John 12:3
Then took Mary a pound of ointment of spikenard, very costly, and anointed the feet of Jesus, and
wiped His feet with her hair: and the house was filled with the odour of the ointment.

MY ALL IN ALL

From being a child, Lord, I've tasted Your grace,
And often in worship looked into Your face.
There found forgiveness and blessed relief,
As I gazed on Your beauty, oh, great Prince of Peace.

The peace that You give me in times of distress,
I can only describe as sweet blessedness!
When sickness is part of the way that I tread,
You come to be near me and make up my bed!

As my tears of grief and sadness roll,
You dry my eyes and You calm my soul.
When desolate, my heart feels so low,
You lift me up and You make me whole!

Before Your throne, oh, Lord, in prayer,
I gladly run to meet You there!
I find in You such sweet release,
You calm my soul and You give me peace.

In all the changing scenes of life,
In joy or pain, in need or strife,
My heart and my soul You still enthrall,
You are to me, my ALL IN ALL.

Psalm 17:15
As for me, I will behold thy face in righteousness: I shall be satisfied, when I awake, with thy likeness.

CHOICE

I choose to give my life to You,
I choose to yield my will to You,
I choose to delight my soul in You,
I choose to live my life for You!

You choose to take me to Yourself,
You choose to let me share Your wealth,
You choose to give me life and health,
You choose to let me be myself!

Lest I should think my choice is key,
I look to the Cross of Calvary,
I see You die in agony,
I know You made Your choice for me!

PEACE

That settled assurance that You're in control,
That wonderful treasure of faith in my soul,
Gives peace in my darkness, peace in despair,
Gives confident hope that You'll always be there!

Peace in my laughter, peace in my tears,
Peace in assurance, peace in my fears!
Peace in provision, peace in my need,
Peace in my hunger, I know You will feed!

Peace in my loneliness, peace in a crowd,
Peace when I'm strong, peace when I'm bowed!
Peace in seeing You work out Your plan,
Peace when "I just can't see how You can!"

Peace when I'm waiting for answers to prayer,
Peace in rejoicing, You showed that You care!
Peace in my sickness and peace in my health,
Peace in my want and peace in Your wealth!

Peace that the Cross showed Your glorious love,
Peace that You ascended to Your Father above;
Peace that You live in Heaven for me,
Peace that Your glory, soon I will see!

Peace in Your presence as in worship I bow,
Peace in forgiveness, Your Word shows me how!
Peace that You're coming back for Your Bride,
Peace that Your glory no falsehood can hide.

A PARTAKER

The seed of Your Word, Lord, You planted in my heart,
You watered it and tended it, You loved me from the start!
You took the guilt and shame I felt and banished it away,
The glorious joy of sins forgiven, You gave to me that day!

When the seed of Your nature took root within my soul,
Your Holy Spirit came to me, began to make me whole.
Once alien to Your kingdom, now a child of God I am,
An heir to Your inheritance, like the seed of Abraham.

A partaker of Your nature, that's Your wondrous gift to me,
As I believe and trust Your Word, Your promises I see.
Obeying what is written there, makes me more like You!
I cannot help becoming, more loving and more true.

Love is who You are, Lord, You're gracious, gentle, kind
Tenderness and mercy in me You love to find.
As I get to know You, Lord, Your glory fills my gaze,
You fill my life with beauty in, oh, so many ways.

Plant Thy Word within me, Lord, that I may bloom and grow,
Sanctify and cleanse me, may I Thy presence know.
Partaking of Your nature, oh Lord, I long to be!
Only as I lose myself, may I be found in Thee!

THE DEBT

As all the days of life pass by,
I look into my heart and try
To show, in all I say and do,
The debt of love I owe to You!

Redeemed from Satan's market place,
All alone and in disgrace;
Yet, though You had created me,
You paid the price to set me free!

You took me home and shared with me,
The treasures of eternity!
You clothed me with a robe and shoes,
And gave to me the right to choose!

A royal ring my Father gave,
To show I was no more a slave!
Instead of shame, I had respect,
The right to use my intellect!

Sin's penalty is now wiped out,
It makes me want to sing and shout!
Sweet liberty and freedom mine!
Your captive, Lord, forever Thine!

This is the debt of love I owe,
How can I ever hope to show,
My gratitude and heartfelt praise,
For mercy shown throughout my days?

If I forgot that I was lost,
If I forgot the awful cost,
How could I look into Your face,
Or put You in Your rightful place?

One day there in the Glory Land
Alone, before Your throne I'll stand;
Then, and only then I'll know,
Just how very much I owe!

Psalm 32:1-2
Blessed is he whose transgression is forgiven, whose sin is covered. Blessed is the man unto whom the LORD
imputeth not iniquity, and in whose spirit there is no guile.

ALL THE WAY

All the way across the valley,
Rocks and thorns on every side,
Through the woods and through the darkness
Where we feared enough to hide.
Following closely after Jesus,
Knowing He would be our guide.

We went up and down the mountain
Looked for all that He had planned.
Tables spread with all we needed,
Glorious provision from His hand.
More than we could even ask for,
All of this to help us stand.

Precious Jesus, lead us onward
To the place of inner peace,
Where You are "Our One and Only"
Where all other conflicts cease.
Grant us meekness like a dove,
Hide our weakness in Your love.

Now that darkest night has passed
Now we've morning light at last,
Coming through Gethsemane
Praying, Lord, Your will to see:
Earthen vessels gladly broken
Our two lives, but love's small token.

LOVE'S PARADOX

It is a paradox 'tis true!
I find myself, when lost in You!
I only have true peace of mind,
When in Your loving heart I find
Completeness, knowing You are mine,
And wholeness by Your grace divine!

To make my heart more like Your own,
You sometimes let me walk alone!
So that I may know there's naught in me,
Of goodness, or strength, or ability!
But, clinging to your Cross I cry,
You wipe my tears and draw me nigh!

To build me up, You bend me low,
So that I may pray, times of hardship I know!
To show me Your mercy, my sin You reveal,
To know Your provision, my need I must feel!
To accept my brethren who stumble and fall,
You show me forgiveness and give me recall!

When I want to build, I must first start low!
When I want to succeed, my heart I must know!
When I want to lead, I must first be led!
When I want to feed, I must first be fed!
When I want to be heard, first I must hear!
If I want to know You, I must let You draw near!

SWEET LIBERTY

Deep within the heart of me,
There is a place I cannot see,
Where Jesus lives eternally,
To give me hope and liberty!

He frees me from my sin and shame,
And gives me life in His dear Name,
I can never be the same,
Nor seek for wealth or power or fame!

He comes to me in my distress,
And shows to me His holiness!
He clothes me with a glorious dress,
His own blood and righteousness!

Sweet liberty is mine today,
No longer in sin's bonds to stay;
Liberty to walk His way,
Liberty to read and pray.

Liberty to do His will,
Liberty to love Him still,
Liberty my heart to thrill,
Liberty bought on Calvary's hill.

Though freedom is Your gift to me,
I do not wish to go out free,
But serve You for eternity;
Surrender is such sweet liberty!

It started when I heard Your Word,
The inner part of me was stirred!
I knew my heart was full of sin,
I needed to be cleansed within.
Now my heart within was fearing,
This was truth that I was hearing!

Then my inner eye could see,
A vision of Mount Calvary,
You gave me gifts of faith and sight,
And made my heart jump with delight!
Those eyes of faith helped me to see,
The eternal life You gave to me!

Your Word has touched my heart of stone,
And now I am Your very own!
You laid Your healing hand on me,
You touched my eyes and made them see.
I've felt Your presence, known Your grace,
I've looked in worship to Your face.

Sweeter than honey from off the comb,
I've tasted Your love, how could I roam?
You always provide my daily bread,
All that I need, by Father I'm fed.
You satisfy my hunger and thirst,
And now I've learned to seek You first!

How fragrant were those words of life,
That came and settled all my strife.
Your Name is like that ointment sweet,
Poured out in worship on Your feet!
It smells so wonderful and pure,
And prompts my heart to love You more!

I've heard Your Word and felt Your touch,
I've seen Your grace, and tasted much.
I've smelled the fragrance of Your love,
That permeates from Heaven above!
Each sense, oh Lord, You satisfy,
Help me Your Name to glorify!

Psalm 32:1
Blessed is he whose transgression is forgiven, whose sin is covered.

I need to be careful of this thing we call pride,
They tell me it comes from deep down inside!
You need to watch out for it also, my friend,
It brings only trouble and grief without end!
This pride, it's rather tricky to see,
Do you think it could bother someone like me?

I know pride will cheat me of life that You promise,
I know it will keep me from real holiness!
Is it pride that stops me admitting I'm wrong?
Is it pride makes me want to sing my own song?
Maybe it's pride that comes into play!
Maybe that's why I want my own way!

Do you think it is pride when I can't forgive?
It might not look good to the folks where I live.
I really don't want them to think I'm unwise,
But why can't I look them right in the eyes?
Maybe if I just forget I'm not right,
My conscience won't ever bring it to light!

Don't you think I deserve more than I've got?
I can't be content if this is my lot!
I'm better than most of the folks that I meet,
It sure isn't fair, Lord, am I indiscreet?
It couldn't be pride makes me think in this way,
It's got to be right to live for today!

This pride is really hard to detect,
It fools me by making me think I'm the best!
I can't follow You, Lord, if I think I am right,
I can't do Your will, Lord, if You're not in sight!
Please help me to look to this heart of mine,
I can't trust my own heart but I can trust Thine!

THE TRAP

Who is that standing at the door of my heart?
Waiting to trap me when I'm not so smart?
He's perfectly willing to wait for a while,
He's not going to rush me, that's just not his style!
He knows what I've read, and prayed, and sung!
And patiently waits for the trap to be sprung!

He knows me quite well, this enemy of mine.
He remembers my weakness, knows I am Thine!
Though he tells me quite often my shame I must hide,
He readily spreads it around, far and wide.
He knows when I confess to Jesus my King,
He'll have no more power to bring suffering!

The trap that he plans is set just for me,
He says that within me, I have the key!
He wants me to think I can cope on my own,
He tells me the Lord will leave me alone.
I know that's not true, oh, heart of my heart,
And Satan's a liar right from the start!

His fingerprints seen on everyone's life,
Deception and secrecy, distortion and strife.
Help me to tear down the lies he inspires,
Help me to put up the truth God requires.
My enemy hates me to read and to pray,
It's only the TRUTH that can turn him away!

I wonder whatever could be his chief aim?
Is he seeking to keep me from riches or fame?
No, he has a much more serious plan,
To prevent my worship and love of the Lamb!
If I worship the Lord with all of my heart
Satan will flee; Lord, how precious Thou art!

MY BROTHER'S SIN

I should not judge my brother's sin,
But, oh, it comes from deep within!
Why did he not obey God's Word?
He must have known! He must have heard!

I would not think the worst of him,
Or blame him on the merest whim.
He is my brother after all!
I take no pleasure in his fall!

I could have gone to him to say,
My friend, I'll pray for you today!
It's only by God's grace I stand,
I'll give to you a helping hand.

I should not think I will not fall,
There isn't any doubt at all,
That when I'm tried and tested sore,
My sinful self comes to the fore!

I would not know redeeming grace,
I could not feel His sweet embrace,
If God had judged me with the Law,
Or laid on me that final straw!

I could not seek for judgment now,
But only in Your presence bow.
My brother's sin brings pain to me,
My sin became Your agony!

1 Corinthians 10:12
Wherefore let him that thinketh he standeth take heed lest he fall.

THROUGH SUNSHINE AND RAIN

Today, on this your most special of days,
We want you to know, that now and always,
You will keep that place deep down in your heart,
Just as you have done, right from the start.

We've cared for you, tended you, watched as you grew,
We've loved you and taught you and prayed for you too!
We've shared days of sunshine and walked through the rain:
Been proud of your achievements and wept for your pain.

Now you have found the love of your life,
Uniting together as husband and wife;
Pledging that you will always be true,
Open and honest in all that you do.

May you have hope when all hope is gone,
May you have joy in knowing God's Son!
May you have laughter to dry up your tears,
May you have faith to calm all your fears.

May you know grace each day that you live,
May you have peace as you learn to forgive!
Love, joy and peace from Heaven above,
Given to you by God's Son who is love!

1 Corinthians 13:4-6
Love is patient and kind. Love is not jealous or boastful or proud or rude. Love does not demand its own way.
Love is not irritable, and it keeps no record of when it has been wronged. It is never glad about injustice but
rejoices whenever the truth wins out.   (New Living Translation)

OUR GIFT OF LOVE

Sweet little baby with wrinkly nose,
Ten small fingers and ten small toes;
Lying there, so cozy and warm,
Free from all danger, fear and harm.

Mother looks on with eyes full of love,
Father looks down on them both from above;
All of the eyes that see him lie there,
Know that he is an answer to prayer.

The gift of life in a sleeping suit,
Beautiful, helpless and ever so cute!
How blessed you are, oh, little one,
With parents who know that God too has a Son!

A family who love and honour His Name,
Who may never be rich or know worldwide fame;
But have more to give than the wealthiest heir;
God has entrusted you to their care.

A family to love you, a life to be shared,
Always you'll know that somebody cared!
You will be safe and secure as you grow,
And gently be led the Saviour to know.

You light up our lives like the rays of the sun,
Our love and our hearts, already you've won!
Our prayers are for you today and always,
That you will love Jesus for all of your days.

61

... AND FOR EVER

SECTION
3

ONE ORDINARY DAY

One ordinary morning I will rise up from my bed,
And come into the presence of Christ, my Living Head.
I will praise Him for His goodness, and kneeling there to pray,
I will ask Him for His blessing on my ordinary day!

I'll rise from my devotions learning something from His Word,
And seek to make a practice of the things that I have heard.
I'll remember He is with me every step along the way,
And seek to live for Jesus in my ordinary day.

I'll eat my breakfast, clean the house, do dishes, make the lunch.
I'll even hang out washing or put flowers in a bunch.
I'll check the emails, read the post, more bills we have to pay!
Keeping me quite busy on my ordinary day.

Then suddenly I'll hear the sound of shofar horn blown loud,
And I will rise to meet Him, my Bridegroom, in the clouds.
I'll see Him, oh, so quickly, in the twinkling of an eye,
Forever changed and perfect, nevermore to die!

I shall not fear to meet Him, imperfect though I am,
For when I see my Jesus, He'll be my perfect Lamb,
His sacrifice on Calvary took all my sins away,
So I can rise to meet Him, on my ordinary day!

1 Thessalonians 4:16
For the Lord himself shall descend from heaven with a shout, with the voice of the archangel, and with the trump
of God: and the dead in Christ shall rise first.

64

THE MARRIAGE

It may be in the morning light,
Or could it be at dead of night?
That I will see my glorious King,
Come for me on angel's wings?

I'll hear the sound of trumpet loud,
I'll see His glory in the clouds!
My heavenly Bridegroom's come for me,
My Saviour's face at last I'll see!

The dead in Christ at first will rise,
Then I will meet Him in the skies!
The Bride complete will go to be,
With her Lord eternally!

The home that He's prepared above,
Has gates of pearl, is filled with love!
Walls that shine with jewels bright,
Streets of gold reflect His light!

He'll draw me to the Bema Seat,
All my life will be complete;
Then search my life and look to see,
The motives deep inside of me!

He'll search me with such tenderness,
And look to see how He can bless,
Someone who failed, felt weak and lame,
But longed to glorify His Name!

The jewels from my earthly life,
The crowns for overcoming strife;
Should I be blessed, should they be meet,
I'll lay them at my Saviour's feet!

Presented to the Father pure,
The spotless Bride will stand before
His royal presence, and adore
The Bridegroom, and we'll love Him more!

The Marriage Supper is prepared,
A royal banquet to be shared;
The toast is to the King of kings,
I'll lift my voice and loudly sing!

"Be Thou glorified and praised,
Oh, Lamb of God, I'm still amazed
That You should stoop right down to be,
Married to someone like me!"

1 Thessalonians 4:16-17
For the Lord himself shall descend from heaven with a shout, with the voice of the archangel, and with the
trump of God: and the dead in Christ shall rise first: Then we which are alive and remain shall be caught up
together with them in the clouds, to meet the Lord in the air: and so shall we ever be with the Lord.

TO BE YOUR BRIDE

Am I to be Your bride, Lord?
Am I to see Your face?
Am I to be Your bride, Lord?
And taste of sovereign grace?

Will You come for me at midnight?
Or will it be near dawn?
Can I see the glow of twilight?
Can I hear the shofar horn?

Am I to be Your bride, Lord?
Is my garment ready soon?
Am I to be Your bride, Lord?
Are there jewels to be worn?

The home that You're preparing,
Is it almost finished, Lord?
A home of love and sharing,
A home of great reward.

Am I to be Your bride, Lord?
Oh, I can hardly wait.
Am I to be Your bride, Lord?
Oh, when will be the date?

May I run to meet You, Lord,
Be it morning, night or noon.
May I give You joy, Lord,
Oh, make Your coming soon!

PATMOS GLORY

Imprisoned here on Patmos Isle
I'll just sit here and rest awhile.
Those lights across the Aegean Sea,
That is where my friends will be!
Shivering here in the bitter cold
Reminds me that I'm getting old:
Too old to work in the heat of the day,
Too old to sleep on a bed of clay!

Over the sea, the churches I cherished,
Every disciple I loved has perished!
Here I am, alone in this place,
I only survive because of His grace!
Surely this could not be in His plan,
The future can't rest on one old man!
All of our dreams have come to an end
I'm sitting here and long for a friend!

It's Your day, Lord, oh, let me see
Your face, the way it used to be,
Before You suffered on Calvary's Tree,
Before You gave your life for me.
Full of love and light and mercy:
Full of grace and peace and beauty.
I was a witness, Lord, to Your glory:
May I be the one to write Your story!

Oh, now I can see You again, so bright,
My old eyes can't stand the light!
Your voice to me is loud and clear:
I'll write Your words as I shed my tears.
A message for each of the churches I love!
Right from Your throne in Heaven above!
You know each one with their faults and their fears
What glory is this? I know You are near!

Lord, I can hardly take it in!
Your judgment falls on a world full of sin.
No good or righteousness left in Your world,
The reign of Antichrist now unfurled.
Before creation, You had a plan,
To deal with the wickedness of man:
Now is the final Judgment Day
When You take control and hold full sway!

Wonderful, this vision of Your glory!
Your Bride is pure and clean and holy.
The marriage supper is prepared,
Great celebration to be shared!
My tears just flow right down my face,
What miracles of sovereign grace!
I'm not alone, Lord, after all!
Before Your throne I gladly fall!

Revelation 1:10
I was in the Spirit on the Lord's day, and heard behind me a great voice, as of a trumpet.

Many Christian people today will say,
God's chosen people have had their day!
They disobeyed God too many times,
He is punishing them now for all of their crimes!
Time after time, God forgave their sin,
Sent prophets and priests to bring healing within!
They repented, but sadly, the change did not last,
Soon they returned to their sin of the past!

God sent their Messiah, but they did not believe!
His love and His mercy they would not receive!
Then He sent His own Son to die on a tree,
To open a fountain for them and for me!
Yes, sin pays wages, of that we are sure;
No repentance means that sin has no cure!
So God left His people to go their own way,
Until Messiah returns, His power to display!

But a promise was made to dear Abraham,
That promise was made by the great I AM;
He keeps His Word, His promise is true,
What He has promised, He surely will do!
One day the Redeemer will come to Zion,
A breastplate of righteousness He will put on!
Men will fear the Lord from morning to night,
And all nations will come to see His light!

"A crown of glory in the hand of the Lord;
A royal diadem in the hand of thy God!"
The Lord will delight in those He loves,
He will rejoice over her, as a Bridegroom does!
They shall be called holy, a people, sought out,
No longer forsaken, no longer cast out!
Salvation comes in the Name of the Lord,
Your Redeemer loves you, He gave you His word!

Our God sent a Saviour to all who believe,
His promise is true to those who receive,
He will always love each one of His own,
He will never forsake and never disown.
Though now He has turned away His face,
From those who are His chosen race,
He will never forget them, He loves them still,
His purpose in them He is bound to fulfil!

We too are chosen and loved by I AM,
We too have a wonderful part in His plan;
We believed and received forgiveness from sin,
His Spirit and life are dwelling within!
Part of His family, His sons and His heirs,
Partakers of His nature, in which we all share!
He's coming for us, of this we are sure,
We believe His Word, our faith is secure!

Isaiah 54:10
For the mountains shall depart, and the hills be removed; but my kindness shall not depart from thee, neither
shall the covenant of my peace be removed, saith the LORD that hath mercy on thee.

THE ANGELS WERE AMAZED!

When the Word was made flesh in Bethlehem's stall,
When shepherds and wise men had all come to call,
When Mary and Joseph gave thanks for His birth,
And words of the prophets were fulfilled here on earth;
When the angelic host sung loudly their praise,
They worshipped the Babe and were truly amazed!

When John baptised in the Jordan one day,
He spoke of the Lamb who would take sin away!
Messiah has come, confess all your sin,
Even I am not worthy His favour to win.
The Lamb was baptised, the Father spoke praise;
The dove rested on Him and angels were amazed!

When they watched Him suffer on Calvary's Tree,
Dying for sinners like you and like me;
The Darling of Heaven, given for man,
Deity stooping to fulfil His own plan!
The Cross between Heaven and earth was raised,
And the angels of Glory were truly amazed!

When the Baby born out of Mary's young womb,
Died on a cross and was laid in a tomb;
Upon the third day, Jesus rose from the dead,
Angels guarded His grave at the foot and the head.
Those who looked in the tomb were transfixed as they gazed,
And all of the angels were truly amazed!

When He showed Himself alive for forty full days,
He proved it in many infallible ways!
He promised that the Spirit and power would come,
Then ascended to His Father and His heavenly home;
A cloud received Him as they all stood and gazed,
And all of the angels were truly amazed!

When the Bridegroom comes to the clouds of the air,
And the saints of the ages rise to meet Him up there!
When the Bride is presented to the Father above,
And Christ will then manifest all of His love;
Throughout all eternity Christ will be praised,
And all the angels will be for ever amazed!

Hebrews 1:6
And let all the angels of God worship him.

THE FATHER TO THE SON!

One day up there, in the Glory Land,
Seated there, at God's own right hand!
The Son will hear the Father say,
"Go, bring your bride home here, to stay!

"The rooms are ready, the time has come,
The waiting time is almost done!
The bride is looking for You, My Son!
You paid the price, her love You've won!

"Go down to the clouds, she'll meet You there!
What joy and love for You both to share!
Seeing Your face will make her complete,
For ever she'll want to sit at Your feet!

"Go now, My Son, do not delay,
Today is Your glorious wedding day!
There's a wedding feast for You all to share,
And Son, You know that I AM will be there!

"Alleluia, the wedding feast has begun!
Today, the praise is for You, My Son!
Your guests are seated, the meal is prepared!
Today it's Your glory that must be declared!

"All the saints of the ages looked in faith to the Lamb!
They believed in prospect, that the great I AM
Would provide Himself as sin's blood sacrifice!
Only Your death, My Son, would suffice!

"Your bride believed that on Calvary's Tree,
You provided a way for them to go free!
Free from the curse and free from their sin!
There was only one way their freedom to win!

"Your kingdom has come, let heaven now sing!
Every knee must bow to The King of All kings!
The praise and the honour is rightfully Thine,
Oh, Lamb of all Glory, Beloved Son of Mine!

Revelation 19:7
Let us be glad and rejoice, and give honour to him: for the marriage of the Lamb is come, and his wife hath made herself ready.